Quiz: 122648

Level: 7.0

Points: 2.0

Great Minds of Science

Galileo

Astronomer and Physicist

Revised Edition

Paul Hightower

 Enslow Publishers, Inc.
40 Industrial Road
Box 398
Berkeley Heights, NJ 07922
USA
http://www.enslow.com

Library of Congress Cataloging-in-Publication Data

Hightower, Paul (Paul W.)
    Galileo : astronomer and physicist / Paul Hightower. — Rev. ed.
        p. cm. — (Great minds of science)
    Summary: "A biography of seventeenth-century Italian astronomer and
physicist Galileo and includes related activities for readers"—Provided by
publisher.
    Originally published: Springfield, NJ, USA : Enslow Publishers, ©1997.
    Includes bibliographical references and index.
    ISBN-13: 978-0-7660-3008-4
    ISBN-10: 0-7660-3008-3
    1. Galilei, Galileo, 1564-1642—Juvenile literature. 2. Astronomers—
Italy—Biography—Juvenile literature. 3. Physicists—Italy—Biography—
Juvenile literature. I. Title.
QB36.G2H52 2008
520.92—dc22
[B]
                                          2007020302

Printed in the United States of America

10 9 8 7 6 5 4 3 2 1

To Our Readers: We have done our best to make sure all Internet addresses in
this book were active and appropriate when we went to press. However, the
author and the publisher have no control over and assume no liability for
the material available on those Internet sites or on other Web sites they
may link to. Any comments or suggestions can be sent by e-mail to
comments@enslow.com or to the address on the back cover.

♻ Enslow Publishers, Inc., is committed to printing our books on recycled
paper. The paper in every book contains 10% to 30% post-consumer waste
(PCW). The cover board on the outside of each book contains 100% PCW. Our
goal is to do our part to help young people and the environment too!

Illustration Credits: Corel Corporation, p. 12; Stephen J. Delisle, pp.
11, 16, 20, 47, 57; Everett Collection, p. 89; The Granger Collection,
New York, pp. 18, 23, 36, 62, 80, 83, 84; History of Science
Collections, University of Oklahoma Libraries; copyright the Board of
Regents of the University of Oklahoma, pp. 7, 50, 54, 70, 73, 75, 87,
95, 106; Jupiterimages Corporation/Photos.com, pp. 1, 28, 93; Erich
Lessing/Art Resource, NY, pp. 56, 104; Mary Evans Picture
Library/Everett Collection, pp. 38, 39, 46; NASA Jet Propulsion
Laboratory (NASA-JPL), p. 101; NASA Marshall Space Flight Center
(NASA-MSFC), p. 41.

Cover Illustration: Jurgen Ziewe/Shutterstock, Inc. (Background);
Jupiterimages Corporation/Photos.com (Inset).

Contents

1

Galileo's Early Years

ON JANUARY 8, 1610, GALILEO TURNED his telescope to the night sky. He had spent the night before looking at the great planet Jupiter. Galileo had seen through his telescope three bright stars lined up close to the planet. He had sketched pictures of them and wanted to see these stars again.

As he looked, Galileo saw that the stars were in different positions than earlier.[1] The stars had moved since the night before! But were not stars permanent and unable to move? Only the planets could move across the sky. Galileo saw with his new telescope something he could not explain.

At this time in the seventeenth century, most people believed that Earth was at the center of the universe. Around Earth circled the sun, the moon, and all the planets. The stars were farther out, fixed in place on a large celestial sphere that rotated about Earth. While the planets moved against the background of stars, the stars themselves did not move. Now Galileo saw the stars moving and began to wonder.

Galileo watched Jupiter and the stars for the next six weeks. He made many detailed drawings of what he saw. From his drawings, he saw these stars were moving around the planet. Galileo reasoned that these could not be stars at all. They had to be smaller planets circling Jupiter. If they were, then not everything orbited Earth and maybe Earth was not at the center of the universe after all.

This was a very dangerous idea at the beginning of the seventeenth century. The Catholic Church and many others said Earth was the center of the universe. All the planets and stars revolved around Earth. This belief was based on evidence supported by the Bible. Nearly everyone believed this theory and to

OBSERVAT. SIDEREAE

Ori.　　　　　　* *○ *　　　　Occ.

Stella occidentaliori maior, ambæ tamen valdè con-
fpicuæ, ac fplendidæ : vtra quæ diftabat à Ioue fcrupu-
lis primis duobus; tertia quoque Stellula apparere cœ-
pit hora tertia prius minimè confpecta, quæ ex parte
orientali Iouem ferè tangebat, eratque admodum e-
xigua. Omnes fuerunt in eadem recta, & fecundum
Eclypticæ longitudinem coordinatæ.
　Die decimatertia primum à me quatuor confpectæ
fuerunt Stellulæ in hac ad Iouem conftitutione. Erant
tres occidentales, & vna orientalis; lineam proximè

Ori.　　　　　　* ○** *　　　　Occ.

rectam conftituebant; media enim occidétalium pau-
lulum à recta Septentrionem verfus deflectebat. Abe-
rat orientalior à Ioue minuta duo : reliquarum, &
Iouis intercapedines erant fingulæ vnius tantum mi-
nuti. Stellæ omnes eandem præ fe ferebant magnitu-
dinem; ac licet exiguam, lucidiffimæ tamen erant, ac
fixis eiufdem magnitudinis longe fplendidiores.
　Die decimaquarta nubilofa fuit tempeftas.
　Die decimaquinta, hora noctis tertia in proximè
depicta fuerunt habitudine quatuor Stellæ ad Iouem;

Ori.　　　○ * * *　　* 　　　Occ.

occidentales omnes: ac in eadem proxim recta linea
difpofitæ; quæ enim tertia à Ioue numerabatur pau-
　　　　　　　　　　　　　　　　　　　lulum

Illustration of Jupiter's four moons from the *Sidereus
Nuncius* ("Starry Messenger"). Because these moons
were orbiting Jupiter and not Earth, Galileo realized
that Earth might not be the center of the universe.

challenge scripture was a serious crime. Galileo could not be silent about his discovery. He wrote and taught about these ideas against the orders of the Inquisition. Eventually, he would stand trial and be imprisoned for his beliefs.

Galileo's Family

Vincenzo Galilei was not a wealthy man. He was a gifted musician and was also a skilled mathematician. His wife Giulia was well educated. She came from a noble family that had lost much of its power years earlier. In 1563, they came to Pisa, a small town in northern Italy. Vincenzo struggled to make a living writing music.

Together Vincenzo and his wife had seven children to support. The oldest of these children was named Galileo. Galileo was born in Pisa on February 15, 1564. Vincenzo later moved his family to Florence. There he worked as a wool trader to earn more money.

Vincenzo Galilei found he could not make a living with either music or mathematics. He was outspoken about his ideas. Vincenzo was respected and wrote a great deal of new music. Music writing at that time followed strict rules. Musicians believed that if they did not follow these rules, their music would sound bad. Vincenzo refused to accept an idea as true just because everyone else believed it. He often experimented with new instruments and new music.[2] He applied mathematics to music and often wrote about these two subjects.

Growing up in this household, Galileo could be no different. He was a curious, red-haired young boy who enjoyed music and painting. He proved to be very intelligent as a child. Galileo was always constructing clever mechanical toys for his own amusement.[3] Vincenzo determined that his son should learn and inherit his business of selling wool. But first, he made sure Galileo had a good education.

When Galileo was ten years old, Vincenzo sent him to a nearby school. The school was in the monastery at Santa Maria Vallombrosa. There the monks would teach Galileo and prepare him for a university. The young boy studied the usual subjects of Latin, Greek, logic, and religion.[4] He became a skilled player on several musical instruments, including the lute. Galileo also wrote a few essays and some poetry.

An Early Education

Much of what Galileo studied was from the ancient Greek and Roman authors. Many of these writings had been rediscovered only recently. Galileo lived in the time called the *Renaissance*. "Renaissance" is a French word meaning "rebirth." During the Middle Ages, most of the Western world had forgotten the knowledge of Greece and Rome. Europe was relearning these ancient lessons, and Florence was the center of this activity.

Most of what Galileo studied was from the writings of St. Thomas Aquinas. Aquinas was a priest and philosopher who lived from 1225 to 1274. He had studied the ideas of the ancient Greek philosopher, Aristotle. Aquinas spent his life writing about Aristotle's works. Aquinas showed how Aristotle's ideas often supported the Bible. By 1500, the Catholic Church had adopted many of the ideas of Aristotle.

Many thought these ideas and theories were the most accurate of the time. The Catholic Church was very powerful and upheld the ideas of Aquinas and of Aristotle. Because Aristotle's theories often supported the Bible, those theories that did were not to be challenged. Educated people accepted these ancient works as truth. Teachers told their students to memorize these old books. Students were not encouraged to challenge their professors or the old writings.

Galileo did very well at his studies. He loved learning new things rather than working with his hands. He found that

Italy in Galileo's time.

Rembrandt painted *Aristotle Contemplating a Bust of Homer* (above) in 1653. The piece demonstrates how the life and work of Aristotle continued to influence not only scientists, but artists as well, for many centuries after his death.

he enjoyed the quiet, thoughtful life of his teachers. His father Vincenzo saw that the wool trade would not satisfy such a skilled and intelligent boy. He decided that Galileo should study medicine and become a doctor. As a doctor, Galileo would not have to worry about money. He could also help support the rest of his family.

When he was seventeen, Galileo told his father that he wanted to become a monk. He wanted to join his teachers at Vallombrosa. Vincenzo was not pleased about his son's decision. He worried about the poor life of a monk. He still wanted Galileo to become a doctor, so he removed his son from Vallombrosa. Galileo was now old enough to enroll in a university, and he was sent to the nearby University of Pisa to study medicine. Galileo did not like the subject much, but he did as his father wished.

2

A New Career

IN 1581, GALILEO ENTERED THE University of Pisa and intended to study medicine. He was already skilled in music and painting. Galileo soon tired of medicine and began to study the subject of mathematics. This subject held a certain fascination for him.

In 1583, Galileo made his first important scientific discovery. The story goes that he was sitting in a church service one Sunday and looked up at a lamp. The lamps in the church hung from the ceiling by a long cord. One lamp was slowly swinging back and forth. Galileo noticed that the swing was very regular.

Galileo used his pulse to measure the time of each swing. As the length of each swing grew shorter, he noticed that it took the same amount of time for each swing. He began his experiments with different pendulums. He made pendulums with various lengths of string and with different weights. From his research, Galileo found that the time of the swing remained constant as the swing grew shorter. He found that the weight of the pendulum did not change the time of the swing. The only thing that would change the pendulum's behavior was a change in the length of the string.

Galileo's Inventions

This important principle of the pendulum allowed later clockmakers to build very accurate clocks. Up until that time, clocks were not very accurate or reliable. But Galileo saw other uses for the pendulum. Galileo used the regularity of the pendulum to design a device called a *pulsilogia*.[1] This was a tool used by doctors to measure a patient's pulse. These devices were soon used by the medical faculty at the university.

Galileo was forced to leave the University of

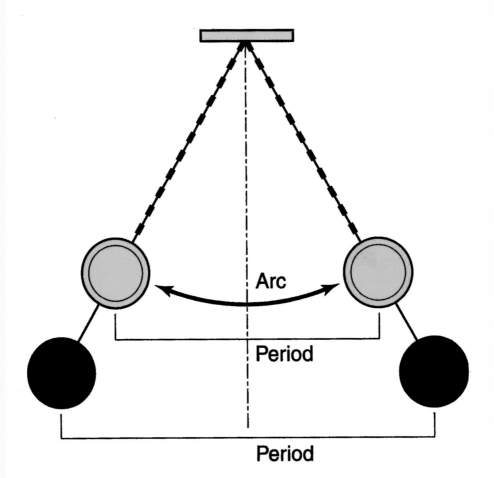

One of Galileo's earliest observations was the pendulum. He noticed that even though the length of a pendulum's swing decreases, the amount of time it takes to complete a swing does not. The length of a swinging object, however, increases the time of the swing, or period.

Pisa in 1585. He lost interest in medicine, and his progress was not good. His father Vincenzo could no longer afford to keep him at school. He did not graduate and had to return home to Florence. Vincenzo was disappointed and worried about how his son would earn a living. He knew well that there was no money to be made in mathematics, but Galileo continued his studies on his own.

Galileo was a great admirer of the ancient Greek philosopher Archimedes and became interested in a problem described in his writings. Archimedes' king was worried that the gold in his crown was not pure. He thought that the person who made the crown used some other cheaper materials. How could he find out what metal was in the crown without melting it down?

The legend surrounding Archimedes tells of the philosopher making his discovery one day while taking a bath. He saw that as he sat down, the water level rose in the bathtub. Archimedes saw that objects in water push aside an amount of water equal to the volume of the object. An object such as a crown would always push aside a certain volume of water regardless of its shape. By finding its weight in air and the volume of water it displaced, the density of the crown could be calculated. Comparing the density of the crown with the density of pure gold, Archimedes could determine if the crown was pure or not. This law that he discovered is today called *Archimedes' principle*.

Galileo developed a type of scale called a *hydrostatic balance*. This delicate balance weighed objects in water and from that, their density

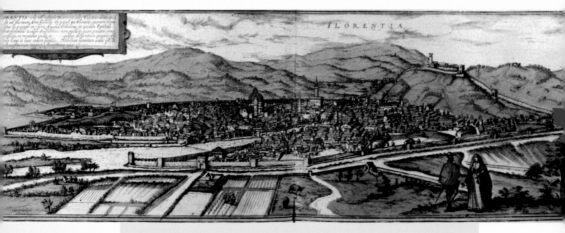

In 1585, Galileo lost interest in the study of medicine. He returned home to Florence (above) and continued to study mathematics on his own.

could be calculated. It was accurate enough to solve the problem written about by Archimedes centuries earlier. Galileo wrote his first scientific paper describing this hydrostatic balance in 1586.

Galileo's studies attracted the attention of a wealthy nobleman, the Marchese Guidobaldo del Monte. The Marchese was a skillful mathematician, and he and Galileo grew to be good friends. He served as Galileo's patron, giving him money to continue his experiments and his writing. Galileo wrote a paper about centers of gravity for his patron in 1588.

Vincenzo was growing old and had not yet made a large amount of money. Tradition said that the oldest son took over the business when his father died. Galileo would have to provide for his family when his father could not. His patron, the Marchese, provided a little money but not enough to support the Galilei household. Galileo began to look for a teaching position at one of the nearby universities.

The mathematics professor at the University

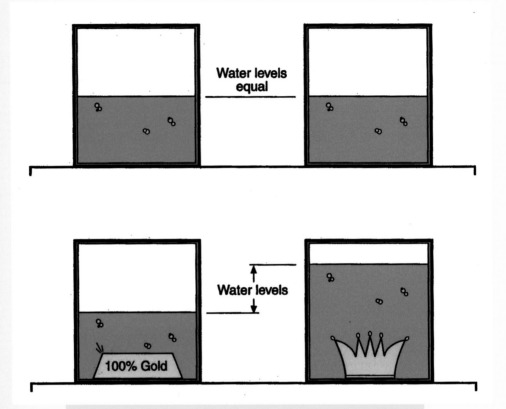

Water levels equal

Water levels

100% Gold

The above illustrates Archimedes' principle. The king's crown, weighing one kilogram (about two pounds), pushed aside more water than a one-kilogram block of pure gold. The volume of the crown was greater than the volume of the gold bar. Therefore, the crown was less dense than gold and so its composition was not pure gold.

of Bologna died in 1587. His position was empty, and Galileo wanted it. He worked to persuade the university to hire him, but they would not. The job was offered to another more experienced mathematician. Galileo went away very disappointed. He tried to find employment at other schools. At one literary competition in Florence, he did very well but was not hired. However, his efforts and talent at this contest gained the respect of others.

A New Job in Pisa

Galileo was discouraged by his failure to find work. He began to look outside of Italy for a teaching position. He thought he might find a post elsewhere in Europe or in the Middle East. The Marchese did not like the idea of Galileo leaving his homeland. In 1589, a position was open for a mathematics professor at Galileo's old school, the University of Pisa. The Marchese used his influence to get Galileo appointed to this post.[2] His appointment was for three years.

The University of Pisa was not a large or

respected university. Galileo was not paid a great salary, but it was the start of a career for him. Here he could work on his mathematics and his experiments. He did not have to spend all of his time looking for employment. Galileo could also gain experience that would help him find a better position later.

Galileo quickly found that he did not fit in with the other professors. He thought they were lazy and arrogant. He said they "were like watermelons in the grass," too big to move and not good for anything.[3] He developed a great deal of contempt for them. Galileo did not believe they deserved the admiration of their students. He did not even like the long robes professors were required to wear. He wore whatever he found comfortable.

Like all the other students of his time, Galileo had been taught the works of Aristotle. It was at Pisa that he began to question whether Aristotle was correct or not. For hundreds of years, Aristotle's theories had not been questioned. Galileo wanted to test these old theories to

To earn money to support his family, Galileo took a job as a professor at the University of Pisa. During his time at Pisa, Galileo began to question the theories of Aristotle.

either prove them correct or disprove them and learn the truth.

The professors at that time did not like discussion or debate outside of Aristotle's theories or outside the teachings of the Church. They used the old texts of Aristotle and Aquinas in their classrooms. The faculty taught science by reading from these books and from commentaries about these books. The students had to memorize these works. They later had to recite these pages from memory. They were not encouraged to question the material or their professors.

Galileo did not like this method of teaching. He did not like it when he was a student and he did not like it now as a teacher. Aristotle developed theories based on logic and reason. He stated problems and solutions in his books without testing his ideas. Galileo believed that theories should be tested, not just accepted. He also believed that the writings of Aristotle may not always be correct.

3

The Leaning Tower of Pisa

ONE EXAMPLE OF ARISTOTLE'S ERRORS is in his theory of motion. Aristotle reasoned that heavier objects should fall faster than lighter ones. This seems to be a very reasonable theory because it follows common sense. A small stone should not fall as fast as a large one. However, Aristotle never tried to test this theory. Centuries later, still no one had tested this theory and the teachers in Galileo's time did not question Aristotle.

Galileo did not like to accept anything without proof. Other scientists of his time had also begun to question the theory of motion as described by Aristotle. One professor, Girolamo Borro, was a faithful follower of Aristotle but believed that his theories should be tested by experiment. Another professor named Jacopo Mazzoni contradicted Aristotle's theory of motion. He said that all objects should fall at the same rate regardless of weight or material.[1]

So Galileo began his experiments by rolling balls down an inclined slope. This setup allowed him to accurately measure the time it took the balls to travel this distance. He tried several balls of different weights from different heights. He collected and organized his data from this experiment. The data showed that heavy balls reached the end of the slope at the same time as light ones. Galileo's theory was different from Aristotle's, but Galileo had proof for his theory.

The other professors at the university did not accept Galileo's data. They still believed that Aristotle was correct. But Galileo had a forceful and determined personality. He did not like to be ignored or told he was wrong. He had the data that showed Aristotle was mistaken. According to legend, Galileo decided to prove his point in a dramatic demonstration. For this demonstration, Galileo traveled to the famous Leaning Tower of Pisa.

Dropping Weights From a Tower

Aristotle argued that when dropped from a height of one hundred cubits, a one-hundred-pound ball would hit the ground before a one-pound ball. This point was easy enough for Galileo to disprove. A cubit was an ancient unit of length equal to about eighteen inches. The tower was just about one hundred cubits tall. He had the perfect setup for his demonstration.

Galileo climbed to the top of the tower and stopped at one of the windows. He brought several small balls with him for his demonstration. Some were made of lead, some of wood, and all had different weights. While getting ready for this demonstration, people gathered at the base of the tower. Some professors came to see Galileo make a fool of himself. Others were just curious. Galileo enjoyed the attention and liked the crowd. He was a showman and loved having an audience to

Legend has it that Galileo dropped several balls of varying weights from the Leaning Tower of Pisa to disprove Aristotle.

watch him perform. When he appeared at the window, he heard the laughs and taunts of the people below him.[2]

Galileo began his demonstration by balancing the balls on the tower's edge. He let them drop together, and they fell to the ground together. The weight or the material of the balls did not matter. Each pair struck the ground at the same time. Even the heaviest ball fell at about the same speed as the lightest ball. Aristotle was proven wrong in a very dramatic trial.[3]

But this was not the time to be speaking

against Aristotle in public. The Catholic Church was not tolerant of new ideas that challenged its biblical authority. It was in the middle of its greatest dispute, called the *Reformation*. The Reformation was a time when some groups were challenging the authority of the Pope and the Church. Groups of people known as Protestants were growing throughout England and Germany. Leaders were taking control of their own countries and moving away from the authority of the Pope.

To counter the Protestant movement, Pope Paul III approved the Jesuit order in 1540. The Jesuits were to consider the Protestant objections to Church beliefs and make reforms, if needed. These men worked for almost twenty years. In the end, they refused to accept the Protestants' ideas and restated the authority of the Church.

The Inquisition

Even though the Jesuits did not agree with the Protestants, they did try to end some of the abuses within the Church. At this time, the

Church was very powerful and some corruption existed from people in power. The Church also had some who sympathized with the Protestants. It was divided with many people arguing over what was right. To end these arguments, the Church established the Inquisition in 1542.

The Inquisition was an organization that made decisions on questions of faith and morality. It examined books and people to see if what they said agreed with the Bible. Sometimes books were condemned for what they included. These books were placed on the Index, the Church's list of banned books. Once on the Index, nobody was allowed to read this book. If people taught from these books, they were put in prison. Some people were even sentenced to death for what they said.

Galileo's fellow professors had seen his demonstrations and the proof that his motion theory was right. Still, they could not believe that Aristotle might be wrong. If Aristotle was wrong about falling bodies, was he wrong about other things? Was he wrong about everything?

And what would the Church say about this? These professors saw the danger of discussing such topics at this time. Galileo was more unpopular now than before.

Galileo wrote about his theories in a book called *On Motion*. In it he described his experiments with the motion of falling objects and his results. He developed his theories scientifically, stating "never, if possible, to assume as true that which requires proof. My teachers of mathematics taught me that."[4] His theories were correct and he had the evidence, but Galileo was unsure of how the professors would react to his work. He was worried about what they might say about his theories. He never published his book.

A New Star Appears

GALILEO HAD A CONFRONTATIONAL personality. He did not have the respect for the other professors they felt he should. He also had a very different style of teaching. Sometimes what Galileo taught got him in trouble. Because of his teachings, after three years his position at the University of Pisa was not renewed.

In 1591, his father Vincenzo died, leaving Galileo alone to support his mother Giulia and his brothers and sisters. He wanted to get a teaching position at the University of Padua. With the help of his old sponsor, the Marchese del Monte, Galileo was hired in 1592.

Galileo in Padua

The University of Padua was one of the greatest universities in the world at that time. It was on the same level as the universities in Oxford and Paris. The University of Padua was in the Republic of Venice, a vital trade center in northern Italy. This area had enjoyed two centuries of steady growth, and the university had a very high reputation.

Padua was then the world's leading center for the new science of natural philosophy. Natural philosophy is what we today would call physical science, or *physics*. It is the study of the matter and forces that make up our world. The branch of science Galileo studied is called *mechanics*, or the science of the laws of motion. The behavior of the pendulum belongs to the field of mechanics.

Galileo stayed in Padua for the next eighteen years. These years were the happiest and most productive period of his life. The University of Padua welcomed new people with new ideas. The professors encouraged their students to ask questions and challenge the old theories. Those teachers that just read from the old texts were ridiculed by their students. Galileo found a place where his style of teaching fit in very well.

He was required to give a lecture to the faculty as an introduction when he was hired. His lectures were always enjoyable and meaningful. They often attracted other scientists and noblemen from all over Europe. Galileo's classes eventually became so popular that they had to be given in a hall that held two thousand people.

While at Padua, Galileo fell in love. Through a friend he met a beautiful young woman named Marina Gamba. Marina was a common woman and Galileo's mother Giulia never approved of the relationship. Giulia was from a noble family and thought that her son should choose someone also from a noble family. However, Galileo loved Marina and together they had three children—two daughters, Livia and Virginia, and a son, Vincenzo.

Galileo wrote a great deal about his experiments and the theories he developed. He taught his students on many subjects including mechanics, sundials, geometry, and military fortifications. Galileo also continued to experiment, building his own instruments as needed. Among the things he built while at Padua were a geometrical compass and the first thermometer.[1]

Talking With Other Scientists

Because his theories disagreed with Aristotle's views, Galileo published very little. However, Europe was going through a period of great scientific discovery. During this time, Galileo began to write to other scientists to discuss their theories and experiments. One of these was a German scientist named Johannes Kepler. Kepler was a noted astronomer, and the two men sent each other copies of their books. Because he lived in Germany, Kepler was outside the direct influence of the Catholic Church. His theories were not censored as strongly as Galileo's theories were in Italy. Galileo wrote to Kepler, "I count myself happy, in the search after truth, to have so great an ally as yourself."[2]

Johannes Kepler (1571–1630), a German astronomer, studied the motion of the planets.

One of the topics Galileo and Kepler wrote to each other about was the correct model of the universe. For thousands of years, everyone had believed the ideas of Ptolemy. Ptolemy was a Greek mathematician and astronomer who theorized that Earth was at the center of the universe. He claimed the sun, the moon, and the other planets revolved around Earth. All the stars were fixed on a large sphere in the heavens that surrounded everything else. Such observations seemed obvious to anyone who looked up into the sky.

Ptolemy's theory agreed with the writings of Aristotle. Aristotle reasoned that Earth must be stationary and positioned at the exact center of the universe. The stars above were fixed in a firmament, or heaven, that revolved around Earth. These stars were perfect celestial objects that never changed. No evidence had ever been found that might suggest this theory was wrong.

A Polish astronomer named Nicolaus Copernicus published a very different model in 1543. Copernicus believed that the sun was at the center of the universe. Earth, the other planets, and the stars revolved around the sun, not the Earth. This model is known as the heliocentric model, meaning "sun-centered." It was eventually named the Copernican system after its author.[3]

By the end of the 1500s, astronomers all over Europe were debating these two models. Kepler had developed theories of motion for the planets that supported the Copernican system, but Church officials and many scientists still would not consider any theory except that taught by Ptolemy or supported through scripture. They believed Earth should be at the center of the universe.

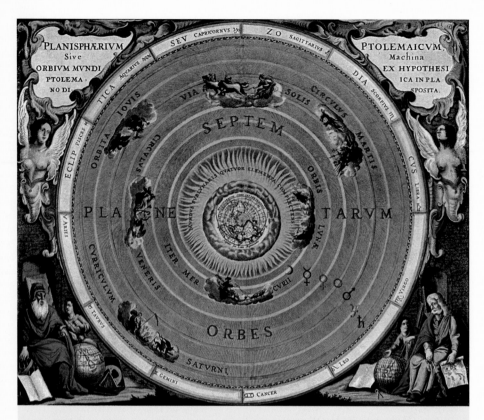

In the early seventeenth century, many people believed in the theories of Ptolemy, an ancient mathematician and astronomer who lived hundreds of years before them. He theorized that Earth was the center of the universe, and the moon, the sun, other planets, and the stars orbited around Earth on fixed spheres, illustrated above.

The Catholic Church was based in Rome and had greater influence inside Italy than in the rest of Europe. The people of Germany were mostly Protestants and rejected the authority of the Church. Because he lived in Germany, Kepler could openly discuss issues like the Copernican system. But because the ideas of Copernicus went against the teachings of the Church, Galileo did not have the same freedom as Kepler to teach and write about these theories.

Copernicus realized that Earth revolves around the sun, rather than the other way around. He did, however, incorrectly place the sun at the center of the whole universe (as shown in this illustration).

A Change in the Heavens

In the middle of all this debate, something extraordinary happened. In 1604, a new star appeared in the heavens. This new star was a *supernova*, the remains of an ordinary star when it explodes and dies. It shined brightly for months before cooling off and disappearing from sight.

Scientists and religious scholars all over Europe argued about the origin and meaning of this new star. Appearances such as these were not new. Supernovae had been seen for thousands of years. Nobody knew exactly what they were or where they came from. Some people thought they were far out in space with the stars. Others believed they were high in the Earth's atmosphere. Some thought them to be angels or omens of evil that was about to happen. A biblical view, not science, is what people believed at this time.

After this star appeared, Galileo went to Venice and gave a series of three lectures about the event. By this time, Galileo had earned a reputation as a noted and respected scientist. Hundreds of people came to hear what he thought about the mysterious appearance. So many showed up to hear him speak that the lecture had to be moved outside.[4]

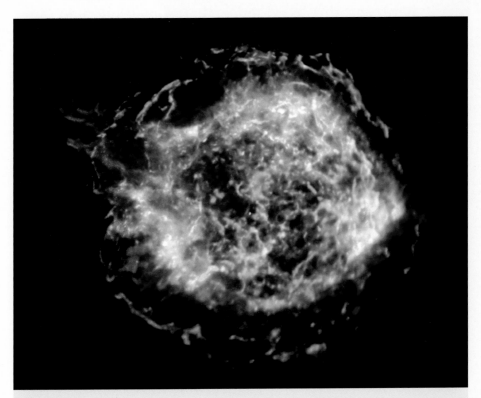

This is an image of the remains of an exploded star, called a supernova, taken in 2004. Aristotle had claimed that the stars and the heavens were perfect and unchanging. In 1604, Galileo witnessed the appearance of a new star that eventually burned out. This led him to believe that the heavens did change.

Galileo believed that what had appeared was a new star, but the actual object was not the topic of his lectures. He instead focused on the flaws of Aristotle's theories. Aristotle had claimed that the heavens were perfect and unchanging. Yet here was direct evidence that something had changed. A new star appeared from nowhere! For a while, it was brighter than even the planet Jupiter. Within a few months, it disappeared entirely.

The other professors were annoyed at Galileo's ideas. The teachings of Ptolemy and Aristotle were still strong, even in Venice. Galileo believed in the Copernican model of the universe but had been afraid to publish anything supporting that theory. At these lectures, he said that the model proposed by Ptolemy was wrong. Here he publicly taught for the first time that Copernicus was correct.

The Telescope

GALILEO WAS NOT SATISFIED WITH HIS salary from the University of Padua. It was a comfortable amount but not great by his standards. He was still supporting his mother Giulia and his brothers and sisters. He had to provide for Marina and their three children. He also had to pay for his house, his servants, and a budget for his workshop and his many experiments. Galileo began to privately tutor the children of noble families to earn extra money.

Many times, Galileo asked the university for a pay increase. Many times, the school officials turned him away, saying, "If Galileo is not content with his salary, he can resign."[1] It would only take one great invention to become rich, he thought. It should be something that everyone wanted or needed and something the noblemen would pay a great deal of money to possess. With this one invention, Galileo could be famous. He could stop his tutoring and devote more time to his research.

In 1608, a Dutch spectacle maker named Hans Lippershey constructed a very curious device. This instrument consisted of two lenses within a long thin tube. Looking through it, one could see objects located at a distance that seemed only a few steps away. It was a crude model and the image one saw was upside down. It was later called a *telescope*, meaning "far-seeing."

Lippershey saw great uses for his new telescope. He applied for a patent but was denied, although the Dutch government rewarded him for this new invention. Others also saw great advantage in the telescope. At this time, Italy was not a unified country. It consisted of small city-states, each ruled by a local prince or duke. These cities were not always friendly toward one another and conflicts arose constantly. The telescope could provide a great military advantage for an army. One could watch the enemy from afar and be warned against an attack. Soon, the telescope was in demand everywhere.

Galileo's Telescopes

Galileo first heard of the telescope a few months after its invention. Word of the new tool spread quickly throughout Europe. Everyone wanted a telescope as soon as possible. Galileo knew a bit about optics and lenses. He took two lenses, one concave and the other convex, and placed them in either end of a small organ pipe. Within a few days, he had constructed for himself a working model of the new telescope.[2]

He presented his device to the senate of Venice in August of 1609. The telescope he had constructed was far better than Lippershey's model. Galileo's telescope was more powerful and, more importantly, the image was not upside down. The demonstration quickly moved outside and across the street. Galileo knew the senators had interest in the telescope for military applications. He wanted to give a practical demonstration.

Galileo took the senators to the bell tower of the Basilica of Saint Mark's, the highest point in Venice. The nobles used the tower to show visitors the beauty of their city. From the tower, Galileo showed them Padua through the telescope, thirty-five miles away. He showed them ships in the Adriatic Sea that would not arrive for another two hours. The senate was so impressed with his device, they immediately doubled his salary. They also made his position at the University of Padua permanent.[3]

Galileo demonstrates his telescope to Venetian nobles. Hans Lippershey invented the telescope in 1609. Using his knowledge of lenses, Galileo improved on Lippershey's invention immensely.

Galileo had found the invention that would make him rich. The telescopes he produced were far better than any in Europe. He continued to experiment and to improve his instruments. The noblemen of Venice were very impressed with these telescopes. Galileo quickly became famous throughout Italy and was rewarded handsomely. With this success, Galileo returned to Padua to visit his family.

This was how Europe looked during Galileo's lifetime. Back then, what is now Italy was a collection of independent city-states.

Discovery in the Night Sky

In the winter of 1609, Galileo used his telescope to look at something other than things on Earth. He climbed to the top floor of his house and looked out over Pisa at night through his telescope. After a while, he looked up into the night sky with his telescope. This was one of the first times anyone had seen the moon and stars with anything other than the human eye.

The first thing Galileo looked at was the moon. Until then, most people believed that the moon was a perfectly smooth sphere; however, what Galileo saw was very different. He saw the moon had a rough and irregular surface. He saw on the moon everything he saw on Earth. The moon had "dark seas and bright lands, oceans and continents, mountain peaks swelling in the morning light, valleys lapsed in shadow."[4] The moon and the heavens were not perfect, as Aristotle had claimed.

Everywhere he pointed his telescope, Galileo found something new and astonishing. He saw that the Milky Way was made up of a large number of stars instead of being one smooth body. Some stars were not one star but were two stars close together. He kept detailed notebooks and drawings of what he saw.

Some spaces in the night sky were hazy

clouds and some were clusters with dozens of stars. Galileo looked at a constellation known as the Pleiades. This group of stars was named for seven sisters in Greek mythology. Only six stars could be seen with the seventh believed to have fallen from the sky. When he looked through his telescope, Galileo saw more than forty stars in this constellation. These stars had never been seen before!

The Moons of Jupiter

Galileo's most important observation came when he looked at the other planets. On January 7, 1610, he looked at the largest planet, Jupiter. He noticed there were three smaller stars in a line on either side of the planet. As always, Galileo recorded their positions in detail in his notebooks. When he looked again the next night, he noticed that these stars all appeared on the other side of Jupiter. This was not so unusual. The planet just moved through the sky as it always did.

The night of January 9 was cloudy, so no

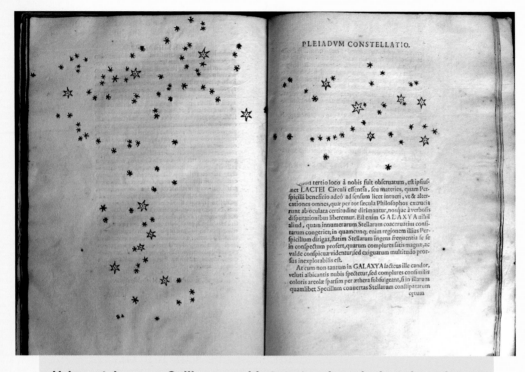

Using a telescope, Galileo was able to get a closer look at the universe and see things that had not been noticed before. Shown here is an illustration of the Pleiades constellation. This constellation was originally believed to contain six visible stars. Galileo found that there were more than forty stars in this constellation.

observations could be made. However, the next night Galileo saw that now there were only two stars but on the opposite side of the planet. The next night, there were still only two stars, and the night after that there were again three. And on January 13, he saw four stars beside the planet.[5]

Galileo realized that these were not stars at all. Jupiter must have four moons orbiting it, just as Earth has a moon. He soon calculated their orbits and saw that they did not disappear at all. Sometimes these moons just moved behind Jupiter and could not be seen. Most important of all, Galileo found something new that neither Ptolemy nor Aristotle had known. There were other objects in the heavens that had yet to be discovered.

Fame and Fortune

NEWS OF GALILEO'S DISCOVERY QUICKLY spread throughout Europe. Since ancient times, there had only been seven bodies that moved through the sky. These were the sun, the moon, and the known planets: Mercury, Venus, Mars, Jupiter, and Saturn. Some believed that our entire universe was built upon the perfect number seven. "If we increase the number of the planets this whole system falls to the ground," wrote one astronomer.[1] Now there appeared to be more in the sky than was first thought.

Kepler called these moons *satellites*, which comes from the Latin word for "attendants." Some scholars refused to believe these moons existed, even when they saw them through the telescope. They blamed it on an optical trick of

Galileo's device. Many refused to look at all. They could not accept the fact that the ancient knowledge was mistaken.

Cosimo de Medici

Galileo published his results in a book called *The Starry Messenger* in 1610. *The Starry Messenger* became one of the most important books of the seventeenth century.[2] This book made Galileo famous all over Europe. It contained a description of what he saw on the moon's surface. In it, he listed his observation of the stars in the Milky Way. He included details of his discoveries of the planet Jupiter and its satellites. He named these newly discovered moons "Medicean stars" in honor of Cosimo II de Medici.

He dedicated the book to Cosimo, head of the noble House of Medici. Although he had a good job in Venice, Galileo wanted to be closer to his family in Pisa. He wanted more time for research and less time required for teaching. His former student Cosimo was now the Grand Duke

SIDEREVS
NVNCIVS
MAGNA, LONGEQVE ADMIRABILIA
Spectacula pandens, suspiciendaque proponens
vnicuique, praesertim vero
PHILOSOPHIS, atq ASTRONOMIS, quae à
GALILEO GALILEO
PATRITIO FLORENTINO
Patauini Gymnasij Publico Mathematico
PERSPICILLI
Nuper à se reperti beneficio sunt obseruata in LVNAE FACIE, FIXIS IN-
NVMERIS, LACTEO CIRCVLO, STELLIS NEBVLOSIS,
Apprime verò in
QVATVOR PLANETIS
Circa IOVIS Stellam disparibus interuallis, atque periodis, celeri-
tate mirabili circumuolutis; quos, nemini in hanc vsque
diem cognitos, nouissimè Author depre-
hendit primus; atque
MEDICEA SIDERA
NVNCVPANDOS DECREVIT.

VENETIIS, Apud Thomam Baglionum. M DC X.
Superiorum Permissu, & Priuilegio.

In 1610, Galileo completed a book called *Sidereus Nuncius* ("The Starry Messenger"). In this book, Galileo published the results of the observations he made using his telescope. Shown here is the title page.

of Tuscany. Tuscany was the province that included the cities Pisa and Florence. Galileo hoped that by dedicating his discoveries to the Duke, he could get a new job in Florence.

His plan worked. Galileo was appointed chief mathematician and philosopher to the Grand Duke of Tuscany in July of 1610. The University of Padua was sorry to lose him but could not match the offer from the Duke. This position had a very generous salary and no teaching duties. Galileo could devote all his time to research, observations, and writing.

Galileo moved to Florence and continued to look at the sky through his telescope. He saw dark spots on the surface of the sun. He also saw that the planet Venus had crescent phases just like the moon. This showed that the planets did not produce their own light. They reflected the light of the sun, just like the moon did.

The phases of Venus led to another discovery: Venus must orbit the sun, not Earth. If Earth were at the center of the universe and everything revolved around it, Venus would always be between the sun and Earth. We could see the planet reflected in the light of the sun but we would only see it as a crescent. Galileo saw that Venus had all the phases that the moon had. More and more evidence was being found to support the Copernican system.

Galileo also saw that Saturn was not one planet but had two smaller stars on either side. They did not appear exactly like moons orbiting the planet. These bodies seemed physically attached to Saturn in some way. Some days, they were not visible at all. "Looking at Saturn within these last few days, I found it alone, without its accustomed stars, perfectly round and defined

Galileo dedicated his works to Cosimo II de Medici (above), who was also the Grand Duke of Tuscany. As a result of his dedication, Galileo was given a high-paying job as the chief mathematician and philosopher to the grand duke and was allowed to spend all of his time on research.

like Jupiter."[3] Today we know these two bodies Galileo saw are actually the rings of Saturn. The rings appear brightly when viewed at an angle. As Saturn rotates, we view the rings at the edge and they disappear from sight.

Galileo studied many different areas of science other than astronomy. He conducted

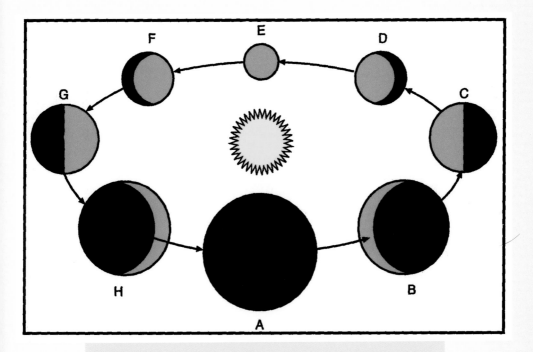

With his telescope, Galileo was able to see that Venus had phases much like Earth's moon. This proved to Galileo that Venus revolved around the sun.

experiments in *mechanics*, the science of force and motion, and *kinetics*, the study of how objects move. His work to make better telescopes led him to study *optics*, the science of light and lenses. He studied the tides of the seas. Galileo also studied *hydrostatics*, the science of liquids and floating bodies. He even published a book on hydrostatics.[4]

Another New Patron

Galileo's work attracted the attention of another wealthy patron. Federico Cesi was a young nobleman who shared Galileo's curiosity about science and the natural world. He collected fossils and built a large private library. Like Galileo, Cesi believed that nature should be studied through direct observation instead of through Aristotle's philosophy.

Cesi formed a small private academy of people like himself. There were mathematicians, scientists, and doctors. They all lived in Cesi's house, and he provided books and equipment for their studies. Everyone was encouraged to teach each other and share their discoveries. They wrote together and sometimes published their ideas.

Galileo was invited to join Cesi's academy and was happy to discover others just like himself. Until Galileo joined, the academy was viewed with suspicion. Some of their studies bordered on magic and superstition. Galileo's presence gave the academy some respect and he taught the other members to be better scientists. The academy even published a few of Galileo's books.

In 1611, Cesi held a great banquet in Galileo's honor. He invited scholars from all over Europe to his villa in Rome. The banquet lasted long into the night as Galileo demonstrated his new telescope. They climbed up on the roof and looked at Jupiter and Venus through the new tool. It was here that one of Galileo's friends suggested the name "telescope" for his new device.[5]

Galileo considered himself a mathematician and philosopher. He studied and used mathematics just as other philosophers did. Ancient philosophers worked theories from their pure logic and mathematics. Plato and Aristotle believed that their reasoning must always be correct. If the physical world did not agree with their theories, this was a flaw with the physical world. Galileo saw his mathematics as a guide, not as a final answer. He believed the observations made of the physical world must be correct. If the mathematics did not agree with the observations, something must have been missed in the calculations. The mathematics would have to be modified until they agreed with the observations.

Spots on the Sun

THE NEXT STEP FOR GALILEO WAS TO visit Rome. Rome was the headquarters of the Pope and the Catholic Church. The Church had great influence over the ruling families throughout Italy. With the approval of the Church, Galileo's fame would be even greater. Galileo was a sincere Catholic and believed his new theories would benefit the Church. In 1611, he visited Rome and spent several months demonstrating his new findings.

The cardinals and other Church officials were greatly impressed with the new telescope, but here a dispute began that would eventually become very serious for Galileo. The Church believed in theories that supported the views of the Bible. In presenting his new theories, the

Church officials felt that Galileo was reinterpreting the Bible. To speak against the Church and its doctrines was called *heresy*.

When he returned to Florence, Galileo began to study the spots on the sun more closely. Looking directly at the sun through a telescope could seriously injure your eyes. One of Galileo's students, Benedetto Castelli, invented a method to observe the sun and these sunspots directly.[1]

Galileo visited Rome to demonstrate his new findings to the Catholic Church. Despite the evidence supporting the Copernican system, Church officials refused to believe Aristotle was wrong.

He could observe the sun safely by placing a sheet of paper behind the eyepiece of his telescope. When Galileo pointed the telescope at the sun, the image was projected clearly onto the paper.

Galileo could see the dark spots on the surface of the sun. He recorded their positions and found that they moved across the sun. They floated and sometimes changed shape, like clouds. These spots all moved across the sun in the same direction and at the same speed. Galileo had several theories about what these objects were but he was not certain.

A History of Sunspots

These sunspots were not an unknown occurrence. Dark areas on the sun had been seen by many cultures and recorded since ancient times, but the new telescope gave scientists a tool to view and study these objects more closely. By the early seventeenth century, many scientists were looking at sunspots the same way that Galileo did. Thomas Harriot of England recorded the first observations in December of

1610. Johannes Fabricius of Germany published the first book about sunspots in June of 1611.[2]

While many other scientists were closely observing the sunspots, Galileo was more interested in observing the new features of Jupiter and Saturn. He was also busy keeping his position in the Tuscan court. Galileo kept very accurate records of his observations of sunspots but did not publish them.

In March of 1612, someone sent Galileo a newly published book about sunspots. The author was unknown, only calling himself "Apelles." He devoted all his study and observation to these sunspots. He claimed to be the first to scientifically observe these objects. Apelles offered the explanation that these dark objects were little planets that passed in front of the sun.

Galileo disagreed with Apelles' theory about the nature of these objects. He saw that Apelles still believed in the perfection of the heavens. Apelles could only think of these objects as new planets because the sun was believed to be perfect and flawless.

He wrote many letters criticizing Apelles's work. Galileo knew that these objects were not stars, planets, or comets. He believed these objects were actually part of the sun itself and moved along its surface. He also saw that they only appeared close to the solar equator. He was not entirely certain what these objects were, but he was certain that Apelles was wrong.

Galileo published his observations in a book called *Letters on Sunspots* in 1613. In this book, he was very critical of Apelles's and Aristotle's philosophy. This book was Galileo's first public argument for the Copernican system of the universe. It was also the beginning of modern solar science and the first account of observations that treated the sun as a spherical star and not as a flat disk.

Apelles Revealed

A year after Galileo published his book, he learned the identity of Apelles. Apelles was a German Jesuit priest named Christopher Scheiner. When Scheiner showed his discovery of sunspots to his superior, he was ignored. They claimed the spots were defects on Scheiner's glasses or in his eyes. Scheiner had to publish his work under a false name.

Scheiner and Galileo had a bitter argument over the sunspot discovery. Each believed that the other had stolen his ideas. Scheiner was insulted and hated Galileo. The dispute between them would last for more than twenty years.[3] Scheiner would even argue against Galileo at his trial in Rome years later.

Galileo's work was more important than just scientific discoveries. He provided ample evidence that Aristotle was wrong about many things. Aristotle believed that the heavenly bodies were perfect and flawless, but Galileo had seen the imperfections on the surface of the moon and the sun. Aristotle said Earth was at the center of the universe, but Galileo saw that it was not. Other moons circled Jupiter, not Earth, and Venus orbited the sun. Clearly, Aristotle did not know everything about the universe.

Aristotle used logic and reason to develop his

theories. Galileo used logic, but he also tested his theories with his experiments and observations. His experiments produced data showing that his theories were correct. He drew conclusions from his observations, not just from his logic. He tried to use mathematics to solve his problems and explain his experiments. This process of conducting an experiment to prove or disprove a theory is known as the *scientific method*. Galileo was one of the first to adopt the scientific method and is recognized today as one of the first modern scientists.

More importantly, Galileo used tools such as the telescope in his experiments. The telescope allowed users to see things much more clearly than with the human eye alone. He wrote that "a magnifying glass is most simply thought of as an additional lens to the eye."[4] Galileo demonstrated for the first time that the human senses could be improved with man-made objects. Using these improvements, Galileo showed they could be used to discover new truths about our physical world.

A Visit to Rome

GALILEO REMAINED A STRONG BELIEVER in the Catholic faith. He did not see any religious problems with the discoveries he had made. Galileo wrote that God revealed Himself to man in two ways, through revelation and through nature. He believed that these two methods must agree. Revelation was personal and came directly from God, but the way to approach nature was through free scientific reasoning.

Most Church officials and other scientists saw things differently. The Copernican system was a direct threat to the belief that Earth was at the center of the universe. Anything that supported the ideas of Copernicus or did not support the evidence of scripture had to be wrong. They dismissed the discoveries of Galileo as illusions. "What a pity that Mr. Galileo has gotten himself involved in these entertainment tricks," they said.[1]

Letters on Sunspots was published in Italian. Scholarly works were usually written and published in Latin. It was the language used by educated people, and all scientific books were written in Latin. Italian was the language of the common people who, as professors thought, did not need to know such things. By publishing his books in Italian, many more people were able to read Galileo's works and learn of his discoveries.

Galileo Writes Letters

Galileo's latest book caused quite a stir in Rome. Debates between the supporters of Aristotle and those of Copernicus began inside the Church. They argued over the evidence put forward by Galileo. In response, Galileo wrote two letters, one to his student Castelli and the other to the Grand Duchess Christine of Tuscany. He hoped

ISTORIA
E DIMOSTRAZIONI
INTORNO ALLE MACCHIE SOLARI
E LORO ACCIDENTI
COMPRESE IN TRE LETTERE SCRITTE
ALL'ILLVSTRISSIMO SIGNOR
MARCO VELSERI LINCEO
DVVMVIRO D'AVGVSTA
CONSIGLIERO DI SVA MAESTA CESAREA
DAL SIGNOR
GALILEO GALILEI LINCEO
Nobil Fiorentino, Filofofo, e Matematico Primario del Sereniſs.
D. COSIMO II. GRAN DVCA DI TOSCANA.
Si aggiungono nel fine le Lettere, e Difquifizioni del finto Apelle.

IN ROMA, Appreſſo Giacomo Maſcardi. MDCXIII.
CON LICENZA DE' SVPERIORI.

In 1613, Galileo published *Letters on Sunspots*. This book served as Galileo's first public defense of the theories of Copernicus. The title page of this book is pictured here.

that these letters would end all arguments over this issue.

His first letter to Castelli addressed the religious arguments against his work. Galileo claimed that the Bible should not be used to deny his observations. He believed science should be independent of scripture. Galileo argued that Church leaders had to agree with physical reality and theory. This letter angered officials of the Church and offended many people.

Galileo's second letter, to Grand Duchess Christine, was a plain statement of belief. He publicly announced that he believed in the Copernican system. He believed that this idea was true and that progress could not be stopped just by banning a book. He wrote, "I hold that the Sun is located at the center of revolving heavenly orbs and does not change place."[2]

He also said that the biblical writers used metaphors and that they were not meant to be taken literally. Galileo even challenged the perfect authority of the Pope. He wrote that the "Holy Spirit intended to teach us in the Bible how to go to Heaven, not how the heavens go."[3]

This second letter was immediately brought before the Inquisition. One of the leading Roman officials of the time was Cardinal Robert Bellarmine. The Inquisition debated the issues raised by Galileo in his letters. Bellarmine defended Galileo and prevented serious action from being taken against the scientist. A simple warning was issued against teaching the Copernican system as fact.

Publicly, Galileo agreed to the restrictions and did not protest. Privately, he was alarmed and wished to present his views personally. In December of 1615, he traveled to Rome to meet with the Inquisition. He spoke with Cardinal Bellarmine, and a panel of inquisitors heard his defense. By this time, Galileo had gained a very respectable reputation as a man of science and truth.

Copernican Theory is Outlawed

In 1616, the Inquisition declared that the Copernican system heretical, or against the teachings of scripture. They called the idea that Earth moves "false and erroneous." Copernicus' book was placed on the Index until it was "corrected," and teaching his model was forbidden. While action was not taken against Galileo, he was ordered "not to hold, teach, or defend it in any way whatever, either orally or in writing."[4] Bellarmine tried to persuade Galileo to abandon his Copernican views.

Bellarmine summoned Galileo to his house to deliver the orders of the Inquisition. The Inquisition sent along several uninvited officials to make sure that Bellarmine was not soft on the scientist. When Galileo arrived, Bellarmine told

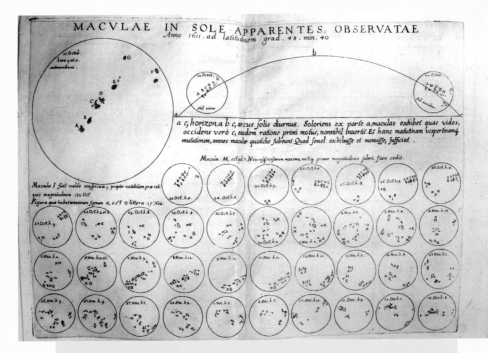

Reproduced here is a diagram which appeared in *Letters on Sunspots* showing features of the sun. The Catholic Church issued a warning to Galileo because of his assertion that the sun is stationary and located in the center of the universe.

him of the Inquisition's decision. He was not to hold, defend, or teach the ideas of Copernicus.[5] If he did, the Inquisition would proceed with their charges of heresy.

Galileo returned to Florence. The decision of the Church was not an official restriction but only a warning. There was still some misunderstanding about the decision between Galileo and the Inquisition. He believed he was allowed to discuss the Copernican model as only a possible theory but not as a real description of the world. Galileo had not changed his mind, but the Church thought he would restrain his teachings and writings.

In August 1618, a brilliant comet appeared in the night sky. It was followed a few months later by two more comets. Galileo began a dispute with astronomers over the nature of these appearances. The astronomers were led by a Jesuit priest named Horatio Grassi. They were debating the origin of comets in the night sky. They believed that comets were solid bodies that came from outside the orbit of the moon. Even though he was correct, Grassi relied on the unscientific evidence of historians and philosophers.

Galileo believed that the appearance of comets was caused by an optical trick of Earth's atmosphere. He published his views in a book called *The Assayer* in 1623. This book ridiculed

In his book *The Assayer*, shown here, Galileo attacked the theories of Horatio Grassi and other Church astronomers. His attacks did not present new arguments to disprove Grassi and the others.

Grassi and the other astronomers. He scoffed at the men rather than presenting arguments against their theories. These astronomers were offended at Galileo's attacks.

Behavior like this was not uncommon for Galileo. He had always been headstrong and was sometimes rude. He felt free to speak his mind and was not very diplomatic in what he said. While some Church officials might have agreed with Galileo, his behavior was offensive and uncompromising. He gradually drove away those who had been his strongest supporters.

9

Galileo's *Dialogue*

CARDINAL MAFFEO BARBERINI HAD AN interest in the arts and in the new sciences. He and Galileo had been friends for many years. They traded ideas and debated the theories of Aristotle and Copernicus. Barberini defended Galileo before the Inquisition in 1616. Galileo sent him copies of each of his books, which Barberini enjoyed reading. His nephew Francesco had been one of Galileo's students years earlier at the University of Pisa.

When Barberini became pope in 1623, Galileo saw an opportunity to overturn the decision of the Inquisition. Galileo went to Rome to visit his friend in 1624. Like his first trip, he brought with him a wonderful new invention. It was called a *microscope*, and it worked on the same principle as the telescope. Using a set of lenses, the microscope made small objects appear large. Just as he did with the telescope, Galileo took another man's invention and made fantastic discoveries with it.

A Visit With the New Pope

Galileo was warmly welcomed by his old friend, now using the name Pope Urban VIII. He amazed the Pope with demonstrations of giant insects as seen through the microscope. But the man Galileo once knew had changed. The Catholic Church was now at war with the Protestant groups in Europe. Urban VIII had to make hard decisions to maintain his control. He wanted to make the Church powerful once again.

Urban VIII would not overturn the Inquisition's earlier decision about the Copernican system. The Pope would not give preference to the views of Copernicus and said his ideas about Earth orbiting the sun must be presented only as a mathematical theory for discussion. Galileo believed that "so long as it is not demonstrated as true, it need not be feared."[1] Ptolemy's model of the universe was still to be held as correct.

Galileo left Rome to return to Florence with praise and gifts from the Pope. Again, there was a misunderstanding between the Church and Galileo. He believed that he now had permission to write about the Copernican model of the universe. He then began to write his greatest book entitled, *Dialogue Concerning the Two Chief World Systems*, often called just the *Dialogue*.

The *Dialogue* was a comparison of the models of Earth's place in the universe. The two models discussed in the book were those of Copernicus and Ptolemy. Ptolemy wrote that Earth must be the center of the universe and the sun, the moon, and the stars all revolve around Earth. This theory was supported by evidence found in scripture and was believed to be an accurate model. Copernicus claimed that the sun was at the center of the universe with all the stars and planets orbiting it.

The book was written as a conversation

Pictured here is the title page for Galileo's book *Dialogue Concerning the Two Chief World Systems*. **Often it is referred to simply as the** *Dialogue*.

among three friends. This was a common method of writing books since ancient times. It allowed the ideas to be presented as a debate, each character taking a different role in the story. Galileo's previous books, *The Starry Messenger* and *Letters on Sunspots*, were considered works only for educated specialists. Even the books of Copernicus and Kepler were too technical. The *Dialogue* was meant to be understood by every reader.

Salviati, Sagredo, and Simplicio

The characters in this book were named after dear friends of Galileo who had died years before. Salviati was the main character and spoke the opinions of Galileo himself. His second character was named Sagredo. Sagredo was to ask questions and prod Salviati when the arguments became too complicated.

The third character was named Simplicio. This word in Italian means "simpleton," and the character was to be a stupid man. Simplicio represented all the supporters of Aristotle. He was based on an old Greek philosopher who wrote commentaries on Aristotle and his theories. Simplicio stood for those scientists and Church officials who opposed Galileo and his discoveries. This character repeated the old arguments of Aristotle and defended the system of Ptolemy.

The discussion in the book strongly supported the Copernican model of the universe. Salviati and Sagredo presented good, well-reasoned arguments. They reviewed the observations made by Galileo. They criticized the theories of Ptolemy and Aristotle. Simplicio looked like a fool with his objections. The conclusion reached by the three men was that the Copernican system was correct. However, at the last minute the characters state that the truth can never really be known.[2]

Galileo finished the *Dialogue* in 1630. He dedicated it to Pope Urban VIII, hoping to have it published quickly. He also included a long preface that stated his devotion to the Church and to the Catholic faith. Church censors

Two of the characters of the *Dialogue* are shown here. Sagredo is on the left and Simplicio is on the right. Simplicio represented the ideas of Aristotle and Ptolemy. Sagredo's role was to ask questions of the other two characters so that they could debate.

examined every book before it was published. For almost two years, Galileo argued with the Church censors. The censors did not want to allow such a book to be published. They suggested minor changes but delayed making a decision.

Publishing the *Dialogue*

Even though the conclusion agreed with the Pope's decision, it was not convincing. The

The character of Salviati, shown here, argued the ideas of Copernicus. Salviati made the ideas of Simplicio, and therefore, Aristotle, sound foolish. In his left hand, Salviati holds a model of the sun-centered solar system.

characters changed their minds at the end for no good reason. The book clearly argued for Copernicus and his theories. It made those who believed the arguments of Ptolemy and Aristotle look like fools. It was a clear violation of the Inquisition's order against Galileo.

On the surface, the *Dialogue* seemed to agree with the decision of the Pope. It presented the Copernican system as only a theory. However, the arguments for this model were strong and reasonable. The logic of Ptolemy and Aristotle did not win the debate. Eventually, the censors gave in and allowed the book to be printed in Florence in 1632.

The *Dialogue* brought fame and praise for Galileo throughout Europe. It was called a literary and scientific masterpiece. It sold out as fast as books could be printed. At first, the Catholic Church received the book warmly. Even the advisor to the Pope said, "These novelties of ancient truths, of new worlds, new systems, new nations, are the beginning of a new era."[3] But Pope Urban VIII had a different opinion.

The Trial

GALILEO HAD SPENT MOST OF HIS LIFE
making enemies within the Catholic Church.
Men such as Christopher Scheiner and Horatio
Grassi were waiting for him to make a mistake.
Publication of the *Dialogue* was a clear violation
of the restrictions placed on him by the
Inquisition. It even went against the decision of
Pope Urban VIII. Now was their chance to settle
the score.

The Pope felt he had been personally
deceived. The enemies of Galileo convinced
Urban VIII that Galileo was poking fun at him
and the Church. The Pope was also under a
great deal of tension from the conflicts with the
Protestants and could not afford to look weak.[1]
Urban VIII ordered the printing of the book

The Assayer, a page of which is pictured here, was the book that first brought Galileo many enemies, as it featured criticisms of fellow astronomers. After the publication of the controversial *Dialogue*, Galileo's enemies would have their chance to attack him.

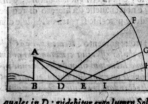

stopped and all copies seized. A special board of the Inquisition was set up to examine the book for errors. This panel was staffed by Galileo's enemies within the Church. No member had special knowledge of science, astronomy, or mathematics. It was even led by the Pope's nephew, Cardinal Francesco Barberini.

This group told the Pope that he was represented in the *Dialogue* by Simplicio. They claimed that Galileo was making a joke of the Pope and the Church. He was also openly supporting the Copernican theory against a previous Church order. Urban VIII decided that Galileo had "ventured to meddle with things that he ought not and with the most grave and dangerous subjects that can be stirred up in these days."[2] The Pope had earlier been criticized as being soft on heretics. Now he was furious and ordered Galileo to appear in Rome.

Galileo was astonished. A request to appear before the Pope was a serious charge. It meant that the accused was suspected of a great crime against the Church. Galileo was a faithful Catholic. He had meant no harm or ridicule by writing the *Dialogue*. He could not believe that he would be considered a threat to anyone.

Appearing Before the Inquisition

Galileo was not in good health and now was nearly seventy years old. He tried to delay the trial or even move it to Florence so he would not have to travel. He even offered to rewrite the book for the Inquisition. But demands by the Church brought him to Rome in 1633. Usually, those who were to be tried waited in prison for their turn to speak. Because of his age and his aching legs, Galileo was permitted to stay at the Tuscan embassy in relative comfort.

He waited two months at the embassy before the Inquisition agreed to listen to him. Originally, the Church had a long list of charges to be brought against Galileo. By the time of his

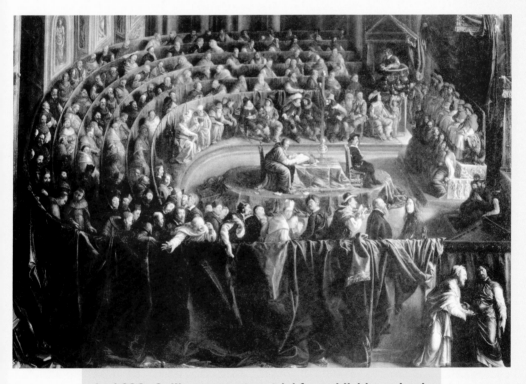

In 1633, Galileo was put on trial for publishing a book that the Church said contained heretical ideas.

trial, these had been reduced to only three. First, Galileo had violated the orders of the Inquisition given in 1616 not to teach or write about the Copernican model. Second, he had treated these theories as real models rather than mathematical ideas. And third, he had actually believed these theories that were considered heresy by the Church.

On April 12, 1633, Galileo was led before the Inquisition. His judge, Cardinal Vincenzo Maculano, sat before him at a large table. Maculano was not one of his enemies. He was appointed by the Pope because he was skilled in mathematics. He had special knowledge of what questions to ask. The inquisitor had a prosecuting attorney on his right and a scribe on his left.

Galileo was asked if he knew why he had been summoned. He replied that it was because of his recently published book. He identified a copy of the *Dialogue* as his own. The decision of 1616 was reviewed as formal charges were read. Galileo was accused of ignoring the orders of the

Church. They produced a letter from Cardinal Bellarmine saying that "the Copernican opinion, being contrary to Holy Scripture, must not be held or defended."[3]

Galileo became very frightened when the evidence was read. He saw that the inquisitor was trying to trap him. The Church examiners said that the book discussed the Copernican theory of the universe. It even openly defended the Copernican model. They quoted material from the book that proved their point. It was printed without permission and ignored the Inquisition's decision of 1616. They said Galileo believed these ideas even though the Church had forbidden them.

At first, Galileo denied this charge. He said that "by writing this book, I do not think that I was contradicting any injunction."[4] Maculano decided to meet with Galileo personally and talk with him about the book. The Inquisition treated heretics harshly with torture and sometimes execution. He hoped that he could reason with the scientist. He wanted to convince

Galileo of his errors without having to resort to these methods.

Galileo's Punishment

The trial would last for more than two months. Over time, Galileo was worn down by Maculano. He admitted that parts of the book could be teaching Copernican views. He may have published it without the approval of the Church. He might have gone too far and disobeyed his restrictions set by the Inquisition. Galileo agreed to confess to the charges. "My error then was one of vain ambition [and] pure ignorance," he admitted.[5]

Galileo was taken to a large public hall on June 22, 1633, where his sentence was read aloud. The formal decree was several pages long and very detailed. It listed his errors in believing that Earth moved around the sun. He was forced to kneel before Church officials and publicly admit his mistake of believing the Copernican model. The *Dialogue* was placed on the Index and copies of the book were destroyed.

An illustration of Galileo late in his life. The trial Galileo faced over the *Dialogue* had left the scientist tired and worn.

Galileo was sentenced to prison in Rome for the rest of his life. Shortly after the trial, the Pope changed the sentence to permanent house arrest in Florence. His trial and sentence were light compared to the Inquisition's treatment of others, but his enemies were satisfied. Galileo and his dangerous ideas were finally silenced.

A Prisoner at Home

AFTER THE TRIAL, GALILEO WAS allowed to stay in Siena for six months, still under arrest. He lived with his friend, the archbishop Ascanio Piccolomini. Piccolomini had sat at Galileo's lectures when he was a young nobleman. He was a great admirer of Galileo and had openly asked to keep the scientist at his home.

The trial had taken its toll on Galileo, both physically and emotionally. He was now sad and depressed and his health was failing. The Church was busy removing all traces of Galileo's work from Italy. News of his sentence was spread to churches and universities as a warning to others who believed in the Copernican model. Books were published that tried to disprove the writings of Kepler, Copernicus, and especially Galileo.

In the meantime, Piccolomini tried to restore the spirits of his former teacher. His home was large and open, and Galileo had many visitors. Piccolomini acquired lenses with which Galileo could construct telescopes. Galileo's interest in physics and mechanics was stirred up again. He was even thinking about writing a new book.

In December 1633, he was allowed to return home to live out his sentence under house arrest. He moved back to his villa at Arcetri, a small town near Florence. Here he was close to his daughters, Virginia (Sister Maria Celeste) and Livia (Sister Arcangela), both of whom were nuns living in a nearby

After his trial in 1633, the Catholic Church tried to remove all traces of Galileo's work from Italy.

convent. Virginia died only a few months after he returned. Galileo's health and mood were worse than ever.

Life Under House Arrest

Time passed and Galileo recovered some of his former health and energy. "He had a jovial face, especially in old age, a stature that was stocky and upright, with a robust and vigorous complexion," as his son Vincenzo described him.[1] Galileo continued to observe the sky every night with his telescopes. A copy of his *Dialogue* was smuggled to Paris for publication in other countries. And he was now working on a new book.

In 1636, Galileo finished his greatest work, the *Discourses Concerning Two New Sciences*. Like his previous book, the *Discourses* again had Salviati, Sagredo, and Simplicio as the main characters. However, this book was about physical science, not astronomy. It left out the theories of the universe that had brought him so much trouble.

The *Discourses* was a book about physics and mechanics. It did not contain much that was not known by Galileo's students from his previous lectures, but it served as a final collection of his work and teachings and his thoughts on many problems. It had a tremendous influence on the growth of science throughout Europe. It would be used by students and scientists for decades.

Because of the Inquisition's sentence, Galileo was unable to publish anything in Italy, but the Church had less influence in the rest of Europe. He sent the *Discourses* to Holland, where it was eventually published. This book was a great accomplishment for the scientist. Facing old age and imprisoned by the Inquisition, Galileo was still working and writing.

Losing His Sight

Galileo could work around the Church, but he could not escape growing old. He developed an infection in his right eye early in 1636. Because he was a prisoner in his house, he could not go out to receive proper medical treatment. By

1638, he was totally blind. He wrote to a friend, "By my remarkable observations, the sky . . . was opened a hundred or a thousand times wider than anything seen by the learned of all the past centuries. Now, that sky is diminished for me to a space no greater than that which is occupied by my own body."[2]

Even blindness could not stop Galileo, however. He continued to work on experimental problems as well as writing appendices for his book. Many students and scientists all over Europe sent letters to Galileo, and he wrote back to them. He now had assistants who read to him and wrote his letters. The Inquisition even allowed a young student named Vincenzo Viviani to live at his villa and care for Galileo.

His house was his prison, but it was not guarded and was rarely watched. A flood of visitors came to see him from all over Europe. The English philosopher Thomas Hobbes as well as the English poet John Milton visited him. They told him his *Dialogue* had now been translated into English. Dedicated students such as Viviani and the Italian scientist Evangelista Torricelli came to discuss new ideas with him. He continued to work even as his health was failing.

Galileo died on January 8, 1642, still under house arrest. He was buried in his own small church cemetery of Santa Croce. The Grand Duke of Tuscany wanted to construct a monument over his tomb to honor the great scientist, but the Pope denied his request. He felt it would undermine his authority to give honors to a convicted heretic. It was not until a century later that Galileo received his monument.

Galileo's Trial Revisited

The Catholic Church felt that once Galileo was dead and buried, his ideas would also disappear. His teachings were silenced and his book, the *Dialogue*, was banned. This man, however, was one of the most influential people in European culture and in experimental science.

In 1744, the sentence against Galileo and the teachings of Copernicus still existed, but that year, Pope Benedict XIV gave permission to revise and print a new edition of the *Dialogue*. The book itself was a brilliant and important work that could not be ignored, even by the Church. On the surface, the "errors" contained in the *Dialogue* were corrected by adding an "if" to some statements. Otherwise, not one word was changed.[3]

The *Dialogue* officially remained on the Index long after the Inquisition disappeared. It was not formally removed until 1822. By that time, science had demonstrated beyond doubt that the once dangerous ideas of Galileo and Copernicus were true. In 1891, Pope Leo XIII founded the Vatican Observatory. Men and books could be stopped, but scientific discovery could not.

Early in the 1960s, a movement began within the Church to reopen the case against Galileo. Confession is a common practice for Catholics, and some then believed that the Church was wrong. They wanted the Church to confess its mistakes and clear the name of the scientist. At the time, Pope John XXIII agreed, but he died before action could be taken. His successor, Pope Paul VI, ignored the issue.

In the 1970s, a new pope was elected, Pope John Paul II. This pope was from Poland, the homeland of Nicolaus Copernicus. He announced in 1979 that the case against Galileo would be formally reopened. When some officials within the Church opposed the decision, John Paul II quoted Galileo himself: "Holy Scripture and nature proceed equally from the Divine Word."[4]

For the next nine years, the Church studied

We now know that Jupiter has at least sixteen moons. The four moons discovered by Galileo—(from left to right) Ganymede, Callisto, Io, and Europa—are named the Galilean satellites in his honor.

the case against Galileo. John Paul II wanted the real truth to be told about the trial. Official meetings were held to discuss the event. Documents were released from the Church's secret Galileo files to be carefully considered. The actions of each participant were examined for truth and motive.

Many members of the Church were embarrassed by the trial of Galileo. The decision was wrong, but they did not want to admit that it was wrong. They had studied the subject and now wanted to bury it again. The Pope would not let them escape the truth. Finally, on October 31, 1992, John Paul II read the findings of the review. The Church confessed that it was wrong to imprison Galileo for his beliefs and admitted its mistakes.[5] After more than three and a half centuries, the crimes of Galileo were erased.

The Foundations of Experimental Science

BEFORE THE RENAISSANCE, THE POPE and the Catholic Church were the strongest powers in Europe. They either ruled or influenced other rulers in Italy and other countries. During the Renaissance, however, some people began to question the authority of the Church. Men such as John Huss and Martin Luther challenged the Pope on political and religious matters.

Others like Nicolaus Copernicus, Johannes Kepler, and Galileo Galilei brought a new way of thinking into the world. They chose to believe what they saw and what they could reason rather than what the Church told them to believe. They relied on facts and observations that were more accurate than ancient theories.

Galileo was one of the scientists who relied on facts and observations, thus bringing a new way of thinking to the world. Shown here is Galileo's room in Florence, with some of his astronomical instruments.

Galileo was among the first to practice the scientific method. The scientific method is the basis for all modern experimental science. It is a simple three-part procedure: hypothesis, experiment, and comparison with data.

First, develop a working theory called a

hypothesis. The hypothesis can be anything that you think might work as a theory but is not yet proven. For example, the hypothesis Galileo used was the official model of the universe as told by the Church. This was Ptolemy's model that said Earth was located at the center of the universe and that all stars and planets orbited Earth.

Second, find some way to prove or disprove this hypothesis. Design a test that will produce some results that can be compared to the original idea. An experiment like this can be as simple as making observations of the moon and planets, as Galileo did. Some experiments are very complex and require a computer to control them. Carefully record all of your data from the experiment.

Third, compare the collected data to your original hypothesis. If the data match up with the hypothesis, then it was correct. Often the data does not match exactly. Galileo's observations of the motion of the planets did not match Ptolemy's model. The moons orbiting

Jupiter and the phases of Venus were used to show that Earth was not the center of the universe. If the hypothesis does not agree with the data, then it must be changed.

Once the hypothesis is changed, the process begins again: experiment, compare, and adjust the hypothesis. As this cycle is repeated several times, the hypothesis becomes better and better. The more experiments that are used, the more accurate a hypothesis becomes. When the hypothesis has been tested enough times, it becomes recognized as fact. When Galileo had observed and recorded enough data from the night sky, his hypothesis became an acceptable model.

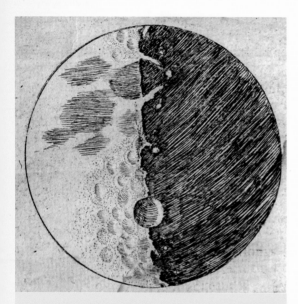

This is a picture of the moon at the first quarter as drawn by Galileo. Some of Galileo's most famous experiments were done by simply observing things that had not been looked at closely enough before.

Moons and Planets

WHEN GALILEO LOOKED THROUGH HIS telescope and saw four new objects orbiting Jupiter, did he see moons or planets? What is the difference between a moon and a planet? Scientists have been arguing this idea for centuries. Only recently has the issue been resolved.

The term *planet* comes from a Greek word meaning "wanderer." It was used thousands of years ago to describe the stars that moved in the night sky. At that time, the Greeks could only see seven objects that moved across the sky. These were the sun, the moon, and the visible planets: Mercury, Venus, Mars, Jupiter, and Saturn.

When Galileo discovered the four moons of Jupiter in 1610, these were called *satellites*.

Astronomers then believed all objects orbited Earth, so "moon" only referred to Earth's moon. As scientists built better telescopes, more moons were discovered orbiting Jupiter and Saturn. The definition of "moon" changed to include objects orbiting any of the planets.

More planets were eventually discovered, including the small planet Pluto in 1930, making the total number of known planets nine and including hundreds of moons. With improved and more powerful telescopes, more objects continued to be discovered. Some of these objects had orbits that crossed the orbits of the larger planets. Some of these objects had irregular shapes. Some were thought to be new planets but were later classified as large asteroids. Some planets were even discovered orbiting other stars.

The discovery of an object named Eris in 2005 presented a problem.[1] Eris was larger than Pluto and shared roughly the same orbit as Pluto. Eris had a moon of its own, just like Pluto did. Both Eris and Pluto's orbit crossed the orbit of the large planet Neptune. Some scientists originally called Eris a new planet. But if Pluto and Eris were called planets, so too could many other objects. New "planets" were being discovered by astronomers every year. Scientists realized that they had no true, clear definition of a planet.

The International Astronomical Union (IAU) is a group of scientists and astronomers responsible for naming newly discovered objects. The IAU met in the summer of 2006 to decide on an official definition for a planet. They decided that an object must have three qualities to be called a planet:

1. A planet must orbit a star.

2. A planet must have enough mass to assume a roughly spherical shape.

3. A planet must clear its own orbit of all other objects.[2]

By this definition, objects like the satellites of Jupiter cannot be called "planets" because they do not orbit a star. Objects with strange and irregular shapes like asteroids cannot be called planets because they are not spheres. And Pluto and Eris cannot be called planets because neither has cleared its orbit of other objects.

Today, our solar system has only eight planets, with objects like Pluto and Eris renamed as "dwarf planets." This result shows that even in our modern age, theories must still agree with the observed physical world. New observations can still change our models of the universe.

Activities

Making a Thermometer

Galileo was the first to invent the thermometer. He initially designed his thermometer to measure the temperatures of the patients in the medical school. He used water in his thermometers, but today we use mercury. Mercury is too dangerous for us to handle.

Materials:

- a small bottle
- a clear plastic drinking straw
- a small amount of clay
- some food coloring
- an index card

Procedure:

1. Fill the bottle about three quarters to the top with water. Add a few drops of food coloring and mix it well.

2. Place the drinking straw halfway into the bottle. Make sure that the end of the straw goes

into the water. Fill in the top of the bottle with the clay, making a tight seal.

3. Tape the index card to the side of the bottle. Mark the water level in the straw on this card with a felt-tip pen. This is the temperature of the room you are in.

4. Move the bottle so that it is sitting in direct sunlight. Let it sit there for one hour. Mark the water level after one hour.

5. Move the bottle to the freezer for a few minutes. Mark the water level.

Objects in Free Fall

Galileo showed an important physical law by dropping balls off the Leaning Tower of Pisa.

The balls he used were all different weights, but they all fell at the same speed. All falling objects are pulled to the earth by gravity. Gravity pulls all objects with the same force, regardless of their mass.

Materials:

- a flat metal baking pan
- a small stool
- several small objects of about the same size, such as a marble, stone, cork, coin, pencil, and a crumpled piece of paper

Procedure:

1. Place the baking pan flat on the floor.

2. Move the stool to the edge of the baking pan. Carefully stand on the stool so that you are looking down at the pan.

3. Take any two of your small objects and drop them onto the baking pan. Make sure that you release the objects at the same time.

4. Note that both objects hit the pan at about the same time. The material or weight of the object does not matter.

Using a Pendulum

Galileo also proved another important principle with his work on the pendulum. He showed that the weight on the pendulum does not affect its behavior. He also noticed that the amount the weight is pulled back before it is released also does not matter. The behavior of the pendulum follows a simple mathematical law that only depends on the length of the string.

Materials:

- a length of string
- a large bolt
- a small screw

Procedure:

1. Tie the large bolt to one end of the string.

2. Hold the string at the other end, leaving the bolt hanging by at least two feet of string. Pull the bolt just a little to one side. Release it and carefully count the seconds as it swings first to one side then back to where it started.

3. Pull the bolt out further than before. Again release it and count the seconds for one complete swing. The length that you first pull the bolt aside should not affect the time for one swing.

4. Pull the bolt out very far, almost horizontal with the floor. Release it and count the time for a complete swing. As before, the length that you pull the bolt aside should not affect the time.

5. Replace the large bolt with the small screw. Repeat steps two through four. Note that the weight at the end does not affect the time for one complete swing.

6. Hold the string at a different place, allowing only one foot for the length of the string. Repeat steps two through four. This is the only change that should affect the time of one complete swing.

Constructing a Telescope

While Galileo did not invent the telescope, he knew enough about optics to quickly make his own. The telescopes he made were the best in the world. He used them to closely examine the moon's surface and to record the positions of the planets for the first time. Some of his optical telescopes are better even than those made today.

Materials:

- two tubes, one slightly smaller than the other so that they fit one inside the other
- two convex lenses and one concave lens, all of about the same focal length

Procedure:

1. Take the smaller tube and place one convex lens inside one end. (It helps to have tubes and lenses of about the same size so that they fit tightly.) If necessary, use a small drop of glue to hold the lens in place.

2. Place the concave lens inside the other end of the same tube. Again, use a small drop of glue if it does not fit tightly.

3. Place the other convex lens at one end of the larger tube. Secure this lens in place with a small drop of glue.

4. Slide the smaller tube, concave lens first, into the open end of the larger tube. Your homemade telescope is now complete.

5. Point your telescope at a distant object and look through the lens at the end of the smaller tube. Adjust the focus by sliding the smaller tube back and forth as necessary.

Chronology

1564—Galileo Galilei is born in Pisa, Italy, on February 15.

1575—Sent to study at the monastery at Vallombrosa.

1581—Enters the University of Pisa to study medicine.

1589—Assumes a teaching position at the University of Pisa.

1592—Appointed as a professor at the University of Padua.

1609—Builds his first telescope.

Galileo observes the night sky with a telescope for the first time, making several important scientific discoveries.

1610—Publishes *The Starry Messenger*.

Galileo is appointed chief mathematician and philosopher to the Grand Duke of Tuscany.

1611—Visits Rome and demonstrates the telescope and his discoveries.

1613—Publishes *Letters on Sunspots*, his first public defense of Copernicanism.

1616—The Inquisition finds Galileo's writings of an Earth in motion about the sun heretical and erroneous and bans the teaching of Copernicus' theories.

1623—Publishes *The Assayer*.

1624—Visits Rome again to see his friend, the new Pope Urban VIII.

Galileo is unsuccessful in his attempt to overturn the earlier judgment against him and his teachings.

1630—Completes the *Dialogue Concerning the Two Chief World Systems*.

1632—After much arguing, the *Dialogue* is published in Florence.

Upon publication, the *Dialogue* is seized and Galileo is ordered to appear before Church officials in Rome.

1633—After delays, Galileo appears before Church officials in Rome.

Galileo is convicted of heresy because of his defense of the Copernican theories. He returns to Florence where he is placed under permanent house arrest.

1634—Sister Maria Celeste, Galileo's daughter, dies.

1636—Finishes the *Discourses Concerning Two New Sciences*.

1638—Loses his sight due to an infection.

1642—Galileo Galilei dies at his home on January 8, still under house arrest.

1744—Pope Benedict XIV authorizes a new edition of the *Dialogue* to be printed.

1822—The *Dialogue* is officially removed from the Inquisition's Index.

1979—Pope John Paul II formally reopens the case against Galileo.

1992—The Catholic Church recognizes the error of its decision against Galileo and admits its mistakes in his trial.

Chapter Notes

Chapter 1. Galileo's Early Years

1. James Reston, Jr., *Galileo: A Life* (New York: HarperCollins Publishers, 1994), p. 97.

2. Ibid., pp. 8–9.

3. Sir Oliver Lodge, *Pioneers of Science* (New York.: Dover Publications, Inc., 1960), p. 85.

4. Reston, p. 10.

Chapter 2. A New Career

1. James Reston, Jr., *Galileo: A Life* (New York: HarperCollins Publishers, 1994), p. 16.

2. Ibid., p. 27.

3. Ibid., p. 28.

Chapter 3. The Leaning Tower of Pisa

1. James Reston, Jr., *Galileo: A Life* (New York: HarperCollins Publishers, 1994), p. 29.

2. Ibid., p. 30.

3. Sir Oliver Lodge, *Pioneers of Science* (New York: Dover Publications, Inc., 1960), pp. 89–90.

4. Reston, p. 33.

Chapter 4. A New Star Appears

1. James Reston, Jr., *Galileo: A Life* (New York: HarperCollins Publishers, 1994), p. 46.

2. Sir Oliver Lodge, *Pioneers of Science* (New York: Dover Publications, Inc., 1960), p. 93.

3. Lloyd Motz and Jefferson Hane Weaver, *The Story of Physics* (New York: Plenum Press, 1989), pp. 19–22.

4. Lodge, p. 94.

Chapter 5. The Telescope
1. James Reston, Jr., *Galileo: A Life* (New York: HarperCollins Publishers, 1994), p. 85.
2. Sir Oliver Lodge, *Pioneers of Science* (New York: Dover Publications, Inc., 1960), pp. 95–96.
3. Reston, pp. 88–90.
4. Lloyd Motz and Jefferson Hane Weaver, *The Story of Physics* (New York: Plenum Press, 1989), p. 36.
5. Lodge, p. 103.

Chapter 6. Fame and Fortune
1. Sir Oliver Lodge, *Pioneers of Science* (New York: Dover Publications, Inc., 1960), p. 106.
2. James Reston, Jr., *Galileo: A Life* (New York: HarperCollins Publishers, 1994), p. 100.
3. Ibid., p. 105.
4. Stillman Drake, *Galileo* (Oxford: Oxford University Press, 1980), pp. 50–51.
5. Reston, p. 116.

Chapter 7. Spots on the Sun
1. Karl Hufbauer, *Exploring the Sun: Solar Science Since Galileo* (Baltimore, Md.: Johns Hopkins University Press, 1991), p. 15.
2. Ibid., p. 14.
3. James Reston, Jr., *Galileo: A Life* (New York: HarperCollins Publishers, 1994), pp. 131–132.
4. Sir Oliver Lodge, *Pioneers of Science* (New York: Dover Publications, Inc., 1960), p. 96.

Chapter 8. A Visit to Rome
1. James Reston, Jr., *Galileo: A Life* (New York: HarperCollins Publishers, 1994), p. 121.
2. Ibid., p. 136.
3. Robert Maynard Hutchins, ed., *Great Books of the Western World*, Volume 28: Gilbert, Galileo, Harvey (Chicago: Encyclopaedia Britannica, Inc., 1952), p. 126.
4. Reston, p. 166.

5. Stillman Drake, *Galileo* (Oxford: Oxford University Press, 1980), p. 66.

Chapter 9. Galileo's *Dialogue*

1. James Reston, Jr., *Galileo: A Life* (New York: HarperCollins Publishers, 1994), p. 195.

2. Giorgio de Santillana, *The Crime of Galileo* (Chicago: The University of Chicago Press, 1955), pp. 176, 181.

3. Ibid., p. 187.

Chapter 10. The Trial

1. Ludovico Geymonat, *Galileo Galilei* (New York: McGraw-Hill Book Company, 1955), pp. 137–138.

2. Giorgio de Santillana, *The Crime of Galileo* (Chicago: The University of Chicago Press, 1955), p. 191.

3. Ibid., p. 240.

4. James Reston, Jr., *Galileo: A Life* (New York: HarperCollins Publishers, 1994), p. 250.

5. Ibid., p. 255.

Chapter 11. A Prisoner at Home

1. James Reston, Jr., *Galileo: A Life* (New York: HarperCollins Publishers, 1994), p. 273.

2. Ibid., p. 277.

3. Giorgio de Santillana, *The Crime of Galileo* (Chicago: The University of Chicago Press, 1955), p. 250.

4. Reston, p. 141.

5. Ibid., pp. 283–284.

Moons and Planets

1. Jane Platt, "Hotly-Debated Solar System Object Gets a Name," NASA Web site, September 14, 2006, <http://www.nasa.gov/vision/universe/solarsystem/erisf-20060914.html> (October 10, 2007).

2. IAU 2006 General Assembly: Result of the IAU Resolution Vote, "Resolution 5A (1)," August 24, 2006, <http://www.iau.org/iau0603.414.0.html> (September 12, 2007).

Glossary

center of gravity—The point on an object where all the weight seems to be concentrated.

concave lens—A lens that is thinner at the center than at the edge. It causes light rays to diverge.

constellation—A group of stars in the night sky that connect to form a picture, usually named from mythology.

convex lens—A lens that is thicker at the center than at the edge. It focuses light rays to a point.

cosmology—The branch of science that studies the origins and structure of the universe.

density—A measure of mass per unit volume.

gravity—The force of attraction between two objects due to the masses of the objects.

heliocentric model—A model of the universe that places the sun at the center with Earth and the planets revolving around it (from the Greek word for "sun-centered").

heresy—An opinion that conflicts with what is taught by the Church. A person who commits heresy is called a heretic.

hydrostatics—The branch of science related to the study of pressure and equilibrium in liquids.

hypothesis—A theory adopted only as a guide, to be proved or disproved later by experiment.

mechanics—The branch of science related to the study of forces and motion.

microscope—An instrument with a combination of lenses used to magnify small objects for normal viewing.

optics—The branch of science related to the study of light and vision.

pendulum—A small weight suspended by a chord from a point so that it is free to swing back and forth.

physics—The scientific study of the natural world, including mechanics, heat, electricity, light, and sound.

Renaissance—The transitional period in Europe between the medieval and the modern ages (from the French word for "rebirth").

satellite—An object that orbits a planet. Natural satellites are also called moons.

scientific method—A step-by-step process that scientists use to test hypotheses with experiments.

scripture—The text of the Bible.

sunspots—Dark blotches that appear on the surface of the sun.

supernova—An exploding star. Some stars turn supernova at the end of their life and shine brighter than other stars.

telescope—An instrument with a combination of lenses used to view distant objects.

thermometer—An instrument used to measure temperature.

Further Reading

Books

Matloff, Gregory L., and Constance Bangs. *More Telescope Power: All New Activities and Projects for Young Astronomers*. New York: John Wiley and Sons, 2002.

McCutcheon, Scott, and Bobbi McCutcheon. *Space and Astronomy: The People Behind the Science*. New York: Facts on File, 2005.

McNeese, Tim. *Galileo: Renaissance Scientist and Astronomer*. Broomall, Pa.: Chelsea House, 2006.

Panchyk, Richard. *Galileo for Kids: His Life and Ideas*. Chicago: Chicago Review Press, 2005.

Internet Addresses

The Galileo Project
http://galileo.rice.edu

Stanford Encyclopedia of Philosophy: Galileo Galilei
http://plato.stanford.edu/entries/galileo

Galileo's Battle for the Heavens
http://www.pbs.org/wgbh/nova/galileoApelles (*see* Scheiner, Christopher)

Index